Listen, It Is Jesus Speaking from the Cross

Mauricio I. Pérez

Listen, It Is Jesus Speaking from the Cross

ISBN 1987446321

1st Edition – March 31, 2018

Seminans

Redmond, WA

© 2018 Seminans Media & Faith Formation
All rights reserved

Printed in the United States.

Maurilio D. Pérez
May 2018

*To a dear friend who has taught me
how, even the heaviest cross,
can be taken up with faith and patience,
one day at a time.
I dedicate this book to Margaret and her family.*

CONTENTS

Preface................................... 9

Introduction............................ 17

Preparation............................. 21

1 Father, forgive them, for they don't know what they do..................... 25

2 Today, you will be with me in Paradise..................................... 31

3 Woman, this is your son....This is your Mother............................ 39

4 My God, my God, why have you abandoned me?......................... 47

5 I thirst...................................... 55

6 It is consummated..................... 61

7 Father, into your hands I commend my spirit.................................. 67

Personal meditation................... 75

Final Prayer............................. 79

PREFACE

For several years now, I've been leading the Meditation on the Last 7 Words of Jesus from the Cross in my parish on Good Friday. That was one of my favorite devotions when I was a kid and celebrated Holy Week in Mexico. The first time my parents took me and my sisters to this devotion, I was 10. On our way back home, my dad quizzed us on each of the seven words. I was able to recite them all.

That year was very special for my Christian faith. Since I was 4, we always attended the liturgies and the Stations of the Cross, so I was used to spending the Paschal Triduum at church. But for some reason, when I was 10 my parents took us to the Tenebrae in the morning of Good Friday, and then to the Meditation of the 7 Last Words after the Stations of the Cross. Then my dad took me and one of my sisters to the Paschal Vigil. I had the blessing of sitting next to my grandma on every liturgy, and she let me read from her missal. I realized that there were some instructions written in red ink that explained what was happening and prescribed how the priest should move along the celebrations. I found then that the celebration of Mass is not something random, and that everything is done for a reason.

I fell in love with the Triduum that year. From that point on, as Lent progressed, I looked forward to Holy Week. We had a routine at home those days. Breaking our family custom, we ate on Holy Thursday in front of a TV set, watching the lovely black and white movie of The Miracle of Marcelin. Then we would go to church to the Evening Mass of the Lord's Supper and would follow the Latin American tradition of visiting seven churches to remember the seven places Jesus was taken during his arrest and trials.

On Good Friday we spent most of the day at church, and at home, we would watch the movies on the Passion that played all day long on Mexican TV. The scenes of the crucifixion always scared me. Good Friday night was agony for me. I had to turn my light on because I could not fall asleep thinking of the crucifixion.

When I was in high school, a new Franciscan friar was assigned as our parish priest. The Franciscans I met before were very good priests. But he was different, energetic, passionate, and with a beautiful deep voice. He preached the Meditation on the 7 Words in a different way, with two harpists or a chamber orchestra playing beautiful music as he asked us to close our eyes and meditate on each of the last phrases Jesus said before he died.

When you're in high school, and then in college, you feel you own the world and nothing or no one can stop you and your dreams. Yet, every time I listened to the meditations of this priest, I would end up in tears. He strongly inspired me to devote my life to evangelization. And I always dreamed of leading one day a meditation on Good Friday like he did.

After I married and moved to the United States, I realized that this was not a tradition everywhere. I asked my priests about it and many didn't even know what I was talking about.

One day, I met a priest from South Africa and we became best friends. I told him about the meditation and asked him if I could do it at our parish. He was very similar to the Franciscan priest I met years ago, and he let me do it. He was sitting in the front pew, with his black habit, kneeling and praying with the booklet I prepared as the rest of the faithful, and from time to time wiping the tears in his eyes, as many others did.

I moved to a different parish and I've been able to continue doing this for a good number of years. This time, I was not planning to. For some reason I cannot understand, less people attend my meditation every year, and it takes a lot of effort to put it together. I was feeling a bit discouraged, but then recalled that no one comes to the Lord unless our Father calls him. Nonetheless, I was busy publishing my latest book in Spanish, *"Judas, ¿Traidor o Instrumento de Dios?"*[1] and I had been invited by my archdiocese to lead a three-day spiritual retreat the weekend after the Triduum. I was very busy putting all this together on top of my daily radio program "Semillas para la Vida" and my weekly program "Pasión por el Evangelio". Not to mention I have a full-time job and a family to raise.

A few weeks before the Triduum, I got an

---

[1] Judas ¿A traitor or an Instrument of God?"

email from my parish asking me if I would do the meditation again this year. I realized God wanted me to do it once more. And it is hard to say "No" to the Lord.

It took me several nights of prayer and writing to compose this meditation. Even fewer people attended this year. But those who did were very attentive and I could see once again many people wiping the tears from their eyes.

When the Meditation was over, several people came to ask me where they could get a copy. One lady who was visiting our parish for Good Friday only, told me that because of the Meditation of the 7 Last Words, it had been the best Good Friday in all her life.

Perhaps God wanted me to do the Meditation once again, so this lady could listen. Maybe there are other people out there who will benefit from these reflections. For this reason, I decided to have it published, so more people can read it, listen to the Lord through its pages, and spend some time in prayer and contemplation.

I hope you will also hear the Lord talking to you as you go through the pages of this small book. Open your heart and listen, it is Jesus speaking from the cross.

INTRODUCTION

After walking with Jesus from Jerusalem to Calvary along the Stations of the Cross, we make a stop. We are standing at the foot of the cross. Witnessing the crucifixion of Jesus is horrific. Yet, we are here because we care. We didn't leave because we cannot let our Lord die on a cross for our salvation by himself. We cannot leave him alone.

There is nothing we can do, as much as we would like, to ease his pain. There is nothing we can do to stop his agony. There is nothing we can do to turn back the hands of the clock and try to save him from the crucifixion. The Son of God came to the world to save us, and he must complete his mission offering his life on this cross for our redemption.

Looking at the cross is painful. We feel tempted to look away. We cannot see a man – who is also God– naked, bruised, bleeding, crowned with thorns, and nailed to a tree. Building courage, we look at him. But the moment his eyes find ours, we immediately look down. We know Jesus is dying for us, and we know we don't deserve it.

We feel tempted to walk away and leave, silently so he doesn't notice. After all, his closest friends have deserted him already. But we just can't. We came here because we care. And we are staying because we love him.

We know we are not perfect, Lord. We confess we have sinned many times. But despite our frailty and limitation, we love you, and we want to listen to your words for the last time.

Speak, oh Lord, your servants listen[2].

---

[2] 1 Sam 3:10

PREPARATION

To prepare your spirit for this meditation, take a deep breath, and let the air out, leaving all your troubles and anxiety behind.

Abandon yourself into the hands of your Father, as the child who confidently abandons himself into the arms of his own dad.

This is your moment. A moment of abandonment and contemplation.

At the foot of the cross, you contemplate Jesus.

Ask Him to send his Holy Spirit upon you to open your ears to listen to his words.

And to open your heart to the mystery of redemption you are about to witness.

Come, Holy Spirit.

Come, Holy Spirit, stay with us.

Come, Holy Spirit. Allow us to feel your presence among us.

Amen.

1ST WORD

FATHER, FORGIVE THEM, FOR THEY DO NOT KNOW WHAT THEY DO.

Father, forgive them, for they do not know what they do.

When they reached the place called The Skull, they crucified Jesus and the two criminals, one on his right, the other on his left. Jesus said, 'Father, forgive them; for they do not know what they do.[3]

Jesus, thank you for your forgiveness. The soldiers who just nailed you to the cross did not know what they were doing. We do not know what we do either. You are right. Neither the Sanhedrin did, even though they knew everything Moses had said[4], they

---

[3] Lk 23,33-34a

[4] Jn 5:36-46

awaited the Messiah and knew when and how he should come. Those who studied Scripture and prayed every day.

Yet, they believed you were dangerous; you hurdled their religious and political plans —you posed a risk to the entire nation, they said. They judged you and condemned you with their political-religious minds, in a country occupied and profaned by the Roman army. You were too unexpected, too amazing, in contradiction with their beliefs.

How well you know everyone, from Pilate to Herod, the Sanhedrin, your own disconcerted apostles, the people who shouted asking for your death! You understand them all and for that reason, you forgive them all. You understand our frailty well enough, Peter's weakness, Judas' weakness, the soldiers' weakness, the weakness of every member of the Sanhedrin, Pilate and Herod's weakness, and your own disciple's weakness, who are not present at the foot of the cross.

Last night, in Gethsemane, you embraced the cross of your silence, of your abandonment. The cross of incomprehension, mockery, wounds, false accusations. You accepted it all in silence, like the lamb that meek and quiet awaits to be slaughtered. And then, you asked your Father to forgive them all.

First, you forgave them and then you asked your Father to forgive them all.

In our case, instead, it is exactly the opposite: we tend to find someone guilty of everything that happens to us; and there is nothing more disgusting than seeing our own defects reflected in others. We condemn others so easily. And we struggle to forgive if we forgive at all. How hard it is to forgive! How hard it is to forget. How hard it is to trust once more.

The wounds don't heal –we don't let them. They leave behind a scar that can't be removed. We condemn everyone before forgiving anyone. Our pride is stronger. And to forgive, we need to become poor and humble, like the humble man who needs to be forgiven himself.

Prayer

Father in heaven, please forgive us.
Because we also have condemned many
innocent people in our life.

We scourge the back of your Son.

We spit on his face even without noticing.

We rebel against his will like Judas did.

We reject his meekness and his silence.

We refuse to understand,
and wish our will is fulfilled, not yours.

Forgive us, Father.
Trust once more our fallen nature.

Trust that after every fall,
we will learn to rise,
as you did on your way to this Calvary.

Trust once more our weak "Yes"
and our conviction that so easily succumbs.

Trust that we will go out
and proclaim your Gospel
if you send us out to do your will.

Yes, oh Lord, trust us always.

Amen.

2ND WORD

TODAY, YOU WILL BE WITH ME IN PARADISE.

Today, you will be with me in Paradise.

One of the criminals hanging there abused him. "Are you not the Christ? Save yourself and us as well." But the other spoke up and rebuked him. "Have you no fear of God at all?" he said. "You got the same sentence as He did, but in our case, we deserved it: we are paying for what we did. But this man has done nothing wrong." Then he said, "Jesus, remember me when you come into your kingdom." Jesus answered him, "In truth I tell you, today you will be with me in paradise."[5]

---

[5] Lk 23,39-43

One of the two thieves nailed to a cross at your side yells at you, "If you are the Messiah, save yourself and save us as well!" You look at him with compassion. You also ask your Father to forgive his ignorance, for he doesn't know you either -he doesn't know God and doesn't fear him. He does not know your face and defies you.

Despair and hatred blend into his words. But thanks to his cry, his partner in crime, also nailed to a cross, speaks up, "Don't you fear God? You, who are suffering the same punishment? We are rightly suffering, for we receive the just punishment to our acts, but this one has done nothing wrong."

This confession begins to shape the first saint in history. "Don't you fear God?". To fear God, not to run away from him, but to know rather that one must seek him like a child, with love and simplicity, being afraid of offending the One who loves us like no one else. And he acknowledges your innocence, "He has done nothing wrong".

How could he know that you are not a

man only, despite his limited heart? He did know and for that reason, he turns to you and asks what seems impossible, "Jesus, remember me when you come into your Kingdom". You look back at him. And enduring this unbearable pain, catching your breath you mutter, yet, with conviction, "Today I tell you, you will be with me in paradise."

And the unthinkable happens! The only saint who was canonized by you happened to be a thief. And we thank you, for this gives hope to each of us.

If it was us, Lord, we would have canonized instead that brave disciple and those women who stay with you at the foot of the cross, shedding upon you their tender compassion. Certainly, we would canonize your sorrowful Mother. But not that thief, whom the Church calls know Saint Dima. It is so hard for us to believe in such a sincere repentance at the moment of death.

We identify ourselves with your parable of the workers of the vineyard. It is not the same working since early in the morning, under the scorching sun. It is not the same to keep fighting and giving up one's life, to have at the end a repented thief making it into heaven the first.

It is so hard for us to believe in forgiveness. It is so hard for us to be merciful. We lock ourselves inside human justice —each one receives what he deserves. Each one harvests what he sowed. Sow a strong wind and you will harvest a storm. We know that. And we can't understand your absolute forgiveness. We hardly accept this coming at the end of the day to receive the same.

How hard it is for us to understand that the prodigal son wasted a lot of the time he could have spent with his father, and he will never be able to recover such time! We sometimes consider the effort, but not the gift, the renunciation over the profit, permanence as a costly stay with our father as opposed to a privilege we receive from God.

Jesus, before you die on the cross, teach us to see through different eyes. From the cross, a pair of eyes looks at things differently, from a better vantage point. Give us a pair of eyes like yours, able to look at things from the top of the cross, from the top of our cross.

Prayer

Jesus is not a wooden carving,
neither an old man who lays asleep,
he´s not the bitter and reclusive God,
faraway on his immense blue.

    Jesus is not a wooden carving,
he´s my Brother, always walking by my side,
talking to me
as he would talk to his best friend,
offering me his life and friendship.

    Jesus talks to me, Jesus calls me,
Jesus, my Brother who loves me.

    Jesus is not the one who watches me
with a somber and angry face,
looking for any sin to heap on me,
a dreadful judge willing to punish only.

Jesus is the faithful companion in my path, that has walked with me with joy and love, and should I sometimes stray away from him,

he will smile and forgive me again.

Jesus talks to me, Jesus calls me,
Jesus, my Brother who loves me.

3ʳᵈ WORD

Woman, this is your son… This is your Mother.

Woman, this is your son...
This is your Mother.

Seeing his mother and the disciple whom he loved standing near her, Jesus said to his mother, "Woman, this is your son." Then to the disciple he said, "This is your mother.' And from that hour the disciple took her into his home.[6]

This young disciple, next to her, is John, your beloved disciple. To whom else could you entrust your biggest treasure?

What a great Mother is yours! She spent her life getting ready for this final surprise. Since that morning so many years ago when

---

[6] Jn 19,26-27

old Simeon foretold what would happen, that day when you were taken to the Temple to be presented to our Father[7].

We look around your cross and don't see your apostles. Where are Peter, James, Andrew, and the rest of the disciples who loved you so much? Where are those who, just a few hours ago, sworn they would never desert you and were even ready to die with you?[8]

Words and promises vanish into thin air so easily. It is facts that remain as true signs of love. Only your beloved disciple is here. If it was us, we would most likely flee as the other apostles, waiting for the storm to pass and then try to go unnoticed.

But John is here. And next to him, your Mother and other women. Blessed women who remain loyal at the foot of the cross, amidst hatred and contempt.

Your Mother is here, enduring the way soldiers and bystanders try to humiliate you. She feels weak and tired as she weeps. She weeps because she loves you –For no mother can bear the pain of a child. And in her case, it

---
[7] Lk 2:35
[8] Mt 26:30-35

is even harder to bear your pain, for you are also the Son of God. She walked at your side for so many years. 30 out of 33, next to you, close to you, allowing you to teach her at the same time she kept teaching you, as all good mothers do. And you, allowing her to form you, as all good children do.

Regardless of your age, Mary looked after you as if you were a young child, even though she never understood the mysterious plans God had prepared.

She weeps but remains firm, standing at the foot of the cross. She looks so weak, yet so strong. She looks so small, yet so great at the same time.

You look at her and feel compassion. You know she cannot stay alone after you leave. She needs children to care for, for she is the Mother. Children who look after her and who allow her to take care of them. Children who make her feel she is their mother, who look for her and seek refuge in her lap, who run after her mercy to regain energy and keep going.

Then, you look at John, and through him, you see all those apostles who are no longer here. You see in him Peter's promise, "I'll give my life for you", and do know they eventually will. They are hiding now, but one day they will give up their lives and die for you. You know they are weak. And for this reason, you know they cannot be left alone. Their blindness could confuse them. They could break apart the group you formed. They are men, and their manly pride can turn them against each other. Even at your Last Supper they quarreled about who of them was the most important of all. They need a mother at their side! A mother who brings them together, who gives them hope when they feel weak, who help them forgive each other when someone fails, and who loves them unconditionally.

Time is running out, so you wait no more. "Behold your mother. Behold your son." What a sublime gift —receiving Mary in our home, in our hearts. So that she's not alone. So that we're not alone. For we also need a mother to gather us, to strengthen us, to give us courage in the darkest nights and peace when troubles don't let us sleep.

Jesus, at the foot of your cross, we ask you to make of us good children of Mary. Help us to open our hearts to her, to embrace her love and to trust her protection. Help us to learn from her to always trust God, despite how difficult or challenging his divine will can be. Help us to learn from her to be humble and pure. Help us to learn from her to remain firm and faithful till the end, even if the end is a cross at Calvary.

Prayer

Holy Friday afternoon,
oh sorrowful afternoon!
Mother, you meet your Son,
your loving Jesus who dies on the cross.

You look upon his dead body;
then, weeping, you look at me.
On Christmas, you gave me a baby,
today I nailed him to the tree.

Who made you carry that cross on your shoulders?
Who made your body bleed?
Who crowned your head with those thorns?
Who made you suffer like this?

You look upon his dead body;
then, weeping, you look at me.
On Christmas, you gave me a baby,
today I nailed him to the tree.

Mother, your soul is mourning.
Yet, mourning beside the tree
that makes salvation possible
to all children of Adam and Eve.

   You look upon his dead body;
then, weeping, you look at me.
On Christmas, you gave me a baby,
the Son of God who has died for me.

4TH WORD

My God, my God, why have you abandoned me?

My God, my God, why have you abandoned me?

At the ninth hour Jesus cried out in a loud voice, "Eloi, eloi, lama sabachtani?" which means, "My God, my God, why have you abandoned me?" When some of those who stood by heard this, they said, "Listen, he is calling on Elijah.[9]

Last evening, just a few hours ago, during the Last Supper, you had told your disciples "Behold, the hour is coming and has arrived when each of you will be scattered to his own home and you will leave me alone. But I am not alone, because the Father is with me." (Jn 16:32). But now we hear you crying out that your Father has abandoned you.

A few hours ago, in Gethsemane, you were

[9] Mk 15,34-35

very close of walking away of your mission and prayed to your Father for this chalice to pass without you drinking from it. But in the supreme example of obedience, to mend the disobedience of Adam, the first man, you surrendered yourself to the will of your Father, "But your will be done, not mine". Yes, we know you learned such prayer from your Mother, who said those words first, in the Annunciation, "Fiat". You even taught us to say that prayer you learned from your Mother when you taught us the Our Father. But this time, the prayer was yours. You surrendered yourself to the will of your Father. Yet now, you feel your Father has abandoned you.

How close you truly are to us. You truly became a man like each one of us, except you never sinned. You are so close to us that you feel abandoned by God as we do many times. Pain and affliction make us forget we belong to our Father and make us forget his unconditional love. Often, we feel as if God has hidden his face from us. And your words become ours, "My God, why have you abandoned me?" We fear that feeling of being alone. We tremble just to imagine ourselves sinking in a never-ending vacuum.

Hanging from your cross, you look at the past 33 years. You remember faces, encounters, healings, manifestations of love. You recall everyone you have loved and all those who have loved you in return, despite their shortcomings. You also see around your cross the deep hatred many feel because of your good deeds, your healings, and your forgiveness. This contempt is the ultimate fruit of envy. You notice in some of the men staring at you the satisfaction of the one who is fulfilling his desire for revenge.

You know how your words irritated many, for they demanded a life change, and the human heart, wounded by the original sin, refuses to change. You see your apostles hiding in fear and feel sorry for their weakness. You see the desolation around you despite the crowd that acclaimed you as you entered Jerusalem a few days ago. You look at your Mother, by herself, and a few other women, present there while risking it all.

You see so many things that you feel profound vertigo in your soul as you wonder, "Does this sacrifice make any sense? Was it worth loving everyone to the extreme? Where is everyone I healed? Where is everyone I formed? Where is everyone I loved? Where is everyone when I need them the most? My God, my God, why have you abandoned me?"

You scream with such a loud voice that it pierces my soul. I would like to tell you, "Jesus, here am I, at the foot of your cross, at your side". I would like to give you comfort at this hour. But I am unable to even console myself! I am speechless after hearing what you just said. I have no words as I see you feeling deserted by your Father. I know you are the Son of God and I am sure you know your Father like no one else. I know you are close to your Father like no one can. Nonetheless, I pray God to give you comfort and strength. And I pray God to give all of us comfort and strength, every time we say the same words, "My God, why have you abandoned me?"

Prayer

Where are you, o Lord?
Where are you?

Let me see you
in the middle of this darkness.

Let me find you
in the middle of this void.

Let me hear you
in the middle of this sorrow.

Let me feel your presence,
close to me, deep in my soul.

Amen.

5TH WORD

I THIRST.

I thirst.

Jesus knew that everything had now been completed and, so that the scripture should be completely fulfilled, he said: "I thirst." A jar full of sour wine stood there; so, putting a sponge soaked in the wine on a hyssop stick, they held it up to his mouth.[10]

Hours have passed, and pain and weakness are taking a toll. The scorching sun and the sweat and blood you have lost make you thirst. Some may think that you thirst for water only, out of dehydration. That kind of thirst can be quenched. But that kind of thirst also comes back. Like it would happen to the Samaritan woman you met at the well. "If you knew the gift of God and who is asking you for water, you would ask him, and he would give you living water."

---

[10] Jn 19,28-29

The thirst that afflicts you is relieved with the eternal life. But not only your body thirsts. Your soul thirsts as well. And as I hear you thirsting, my soul breaks into pieces. You thirst for me, of my commitment, of the water that is hidden in the deepest corner of my well. You thirst for that water that I keep to myself only and never share, not even with you, whom my soul thirsts for. I keep your water to myself and share it with no one.

And that's not it. With your eyes, you look at me, and with your eyebrows ask me to follow your sight. You stare at all those who thirst, at my home, at work, at school, at church, in the streets. You tell me then, "they all thirst". They thirst for your love, they thirst for your time, they thirst for your patience, they thirst for your forgiveness, they thirst for your kindness, they thirst for the best of yourself, they thirst for the talents my Father in heaven gave you, they thirst for your faith, they thirst for your hope, they thirst for your mercy."

I know, Lord Jesus. I know. I know people need me, but I keep my water to myself, hidden in the deepest corner of my well. I would like to turn my well into a spring of living water, but my human weakness, my selfishness, and my pride won't let me. Because my weakness, my selfishness, and my pride have dried out my well.

Prayer

Pour your living water into my well,
o Jesus.

Pour your living water
and my dry well will overflow.

Help me to open the gates of my heart,
and a spring of living water will flow.

Help me, Jesus, to quench the thirst
that afflicts my brothers and sisters.

Help me, Jesus, to never again
keep the water in my well to myself.

Help me to understand
that by keeping the water to myself,
this water becomes stale
and evaporates into thin air,
drying out my well,
drying out my soul,
drying out my heart.

Jesus, you are a spring of living water.

Amen.

6ᵀᴴ WORD

It is consummated.

It is consummated.

After Jesus had taken the sour wine, he said, "It is consummated."[11]

At the foot of the cross, looking at you, everything seems lost. Yet, once more, your words amaze us. Everything is consummated while you seem to be the ultimate failure. You are dying, you are alone, your followers have vanished, soldiers mock you, the holy men of the Sanhedrin rejoice in your torment, you are wounded, and about to die.

And as hard as our naïve heart would like, no legion of angels come to rescue you from death. How can you say that it is consummated? It is hard to understand what

---

[11]Jn 19,30a

you are saying. It is hard to accept this hour, which doesn't match our plans, calculations, and aspirations. The time among us has been so little. Three years only. If you had stayed longer, you could have taught us more about your Father, you could have healed more people and you could have turned more people into your disciples.

But it's been three years only. Three years of teachings, indeed. But thirty of mysterious silence and unanswered questions.

Yet, your words express conviction, "It is consummated".

Perhaps if we look ahead and peep into your empty sepulcher we will understand this better. But it is still Good Friday and the tears in our eyes don't let us reach that far. When you say it is consummated you are announcing you are about to leave, you are about to die. Hearing you say this makes us tremble.

Then we look at our own life and wonder, when will we be ready to declare with conviction, "It is consummated"? We live complaining that time passes rapidly, that life is short, that we always need more time, we keep running and rushing and are never satisfied. We want more and more and yet more and never appreciate what we have.

To you, fulfilling your Father's will is enough. But we don't know how to listen, we don't know how to be obedient. Yes, we seek God in our lives and wish to fulfill his will, but we spend more time seeking ourselves and doing all we can to fulfill our own will. We earnestly pursue success, glory, triumph, and the wide way. We step back at the cross, we rebel at the cross the minute it hurts our skin, we refuse to fail, and we refuse to die. If we could only understand that our life will be fulfilled only when we fulfill God's will, like you.

Hymn

Were you there
when they crucified my Lord?
Were you there
when they crucified my Lord?
Oh! Sometimes it causes me to tremble,
tremble, tremble.
Were you there
when they crucified my Lord?

Were you there
when they nailed him to the tree?
Were you there
when they nailed him to the tree?
Oh! Sometimes it causes me to tremble,
tremble, tremble.
Were you there
when they nailed him to the tree?

Were you there
when they laid him in the tomb?
Were you there
when they laid him in the tomb?
Oh! Sometimes it causes me to tremble,
tremble, tremble.
    Were you there
when they laid him in the tomb?

7ᵀᴴ WORD

Father, into your hands I commend my spirit.

Father, into your hands I commend my spirit.

It was now about the sixth hour and the sun's light failed, so that darkness came over the whole land until the ninth hour. The veil of the Sanctuary was torn right down the middle. Jesus cried out in a loud voice saying, "Father, into your hands I commend my spirit." With these words he breathed his last.[12]

Thank you, Jesus, for your faith, for your hope, for your unconditional love to your Father. Yes. After all, what is left in this world but trusting God?

The last words said by Jesus are a loud cry of supreme and total entrustment to God. "Father, into your hands I commend my

---

[12] Lk 23,44-46

spirit". This prayer expresses the full awareness that, in reality, he had not been abandoned. The initial invocation — "Father" — recalls his first declaration when he was 12. At that time, he had stayed for three days in the Temple of Jerusalem. Its veil now turns in two. And when his parents found him back then, they told Jesus of their anxiety, and he answered: "How is it that you sought me? Did you not know that I must be in my Father's house?"[13]

From the beginning to the end of his life on Earth, it's been his unique relationship with the Father what has fully determined Jesus' feelings, words, and actions. On the Cross this afternoon, he has lived to the full, in love, this filial relationship he has with God which gives life to his prayer.

The words spoken by Jesus after his invocation, "Father", borrow a sentence from Psalm 31[30]: "into your hands I commend my spirit"[14] Yet, Jesus is not merely citing the psalm, but rather expressing a firm decision: Jesus "offers" himself to the Father in an act of total abandonment. These words are a prayer of total entrustment in God's love.

[13] Lk 2:49
[14] Ps 31[30]:6

Jesus' prayer as he faces death is dramatic as it is for all of us. But, at the same time, Jesus said these words with that deep calmness that is born from trusting our Father and from the desire to commend oneself totally to him.

In Gethsemane, when he had begun his final struggle and his most intense prayer and was about to be "delivered into the hands of men"[15], his sweat had become "like great drops of blood falling down upon the ground."[16] Nevertheless, his heart was fully obedient to the Father's will, and because of this, "an angel from heaven" came to strengthen him[17]. Now, in his last moments, Jesus turns to the Father, into whose hands he really commends his whole life.

Before starting out on his journey towards Jerusalem, Jesus had insisted to his disciples: "Let these words sink into your ears; for the Son of Man is to be delivered into the hands of men."[18]

Now that life is about to finish, he seals his last decision in prayer: Jesus let himself be delivered "into the hands of men", but it is

---

[15] Lk 9:44
[16] Lk 22:44
[17] Lk 22:42-43
[18] Lk 9:44

into the hands of his Father that he places his spirit; thus — as the John the Evangelist affirms — all was finished, the supreme act of love was carried to the end, to the limit and even beyond.

- - - - - - - - - -

The words of Jesus on the Cross at the last moments of his earthly life offer us demanding instructions for our prayers, but they also open us to serene trust and firm hope. Jesus, who asks the Father to forgive those who are crucifying him, invites us to take the difficult step of also praying for those who wrong us, who have injured us. The difficult step of being able to forgive them all, so that God's light may illuminate their hearts; and he invites us to live in our prayers the same attitude of mercy and love with which God treats us; "forgive us our trespasses as we forgive those who trespass against us", we say every day in the Lord's prayer.

At the same time, Jesus, who at the supreme moment of death entrusts himself totally into the hands of God the Father, communicates to us the certainty that, regardless how harsh the trial is, regardless how difficult problems are, regardless how painful suffering can be, we shall never fall off God's hands –those hands that created us, that sustain us and that accompany us on our way through life, because they are moved by an infinite and faithful love.

Prayer

Here we are Lord, in your presence.

We are here
to commend our life into your hands.

To commend into your hands
our happiness, our sorrow, and our hope.

Today, into your hands
we commend the life of each of us,
until its final end,
with its sweet moments
and its bitter hours.

With you, Jesus,
we want to repeat forever
the words you said to your Father:
"Into your hands, I commend my life,
so your holy will may be fulfilled."

Amen.

PERSONAL MEDITATION

Jesus has died. To conclude your meditation, take some time to contemplate him hanging from the cross.

Close your eyes and spend this moment at the foot of the cross, looking at Jesus with the eyes of your heart. This is an intimate moment between you and him.

In response to his words, tell Jesus what your heart dictates. Talk to him about each one in your family, especially the one that at this moment needs him the most.

If you have no words to say, that is fine, just contemplate him in silence. It is only you and him, face to face.

FINAL PRAYER

Grateful to our Lord for his sacrifice on the cross, stand and give him thanks for every word he said:

Thank you, Lord.
We need to say we are grateful.

Your life gives meaning to our life,
and your agony helps us understand
that all suffering
is the beginning of redemption.

We thank you for the forgiveness
you gained for us from our Father.

We thank you
for having always the last word,
opening the doors of your Paradise to us.

We thank you for entrusting our Church
to the maternal care
of your blessed Mother Mary.

We thank you for sharing the loneliness
we sometimes experience at home,
and for redeeming us from it.

Allow us to care always
about the thirst of everyone around us,
and to quench it
not with bitter gall and vinegar,
but with the refreshing water
of our love, of our service, of our time.

Allow each of us
to walk always close to you,
so when we reach the sunset of our life,
we can close our eyes with serenity
knowing that our personal mission
has been consummated.

With you, we commend today our life
into the hands of our Father.

From here on,
back in our daily life,
we will bear our cross.

We humbly and sweetly embrace it.

We know that you are here with us
helping to carry it on our shoulders.

Grant us also the wisdom and vision to see,
understand and help others
carry their crosses in life.

This will become also a way for us
to love our neighbor as you have loved us.

By dying to ourselves every day,
may we attain the new life
in you with the Father and the Holy Spirit.

Amen.

Other Titles by Mauricio I. Pérez

All available in Kindle and paperback

In English

At the Foot of the Cross

Our Family at the Foot of the Cross

In Spanish

666 El Criptograma Apocalíptico
Best seller

Sucedió en Jerusalén
Best seller

Judas ¿Traidor o Instrumento de Dios?

Por los Caminos de la Fe

Nuestra Familia al Pie de la Cruz

Todo lo Puedo
en Aquel que me Conforta

Be passionate about our faith!

www.seminans.org

Made in the USA
Columbia, SC
01 June 2018